THE ARMOR OF GOD

A Children's Bible Study in Ephesians 6:10-18

by

David Walters

Illustrated by Dave Odell

Graphics Design and Layout by Judith A. Gilbert

Published by
GOOD NEWS FELLOWSHIP MINISTRIES
220 Sleepy Creek Rd..
Macon GA. 31210
Phone: (478)757-8071
Fax: (478)757-0136
E-mail:goodnews@reynoldscable.net
http//:www.goodnews.netministries.org/

International Standard Book Number: 978-0-938558-52-1

These are five more Children's Bible Study Books available

Fact or Fantasy - Illustrated Children's Study on Christian apologetics (For children ages 8 - 15 years)

The Fruit of the Spirit - Children's Illustrated Study on bearing fruit (For children ages 6 - 15 years)

Being a Christian - Illustrated Children's Study on being a Christian (For parents, teachers & children of all ages)

Children's Prayer Manual – Children's Illustrated Study on prayer (ages 7-14 years).

The Gifts of the Spirit – Children's Illustrated Study on the Gifts of the Spirit (ages 8 -adults)

Other Titles by David Walters

Kids in Combat - Training children & youth to be powerful for God. (For parents, teachers & youth pastors)

Equipping the Younger Saints - Teaching spiritual gifts to children & youth. (For parents, teachers and youth pastors)

Children Aflame - Amazing accounts of children from the journals of the great Methodist preacher John Wesley in the 1700's and David's own accounts with children and youth.

Worship fur Dummies – Is worship limited to Sunday morning worship time? Real worship is around the kitchen sink? Does worship always have to be with music? What is true worship? Are worship leaders biblical?

Radical Living in a Godless Society - Our Society targets our children & youth. How do we cope with this situation?

The Book of Funtastic Adventures - David's grandsons have amazing, hilarious adventures as junior Jedi Knights (Padawans) as they meet famous characters from the book, cartoon, & movies, plus super heroes. Stories with lessons on dealing with sibling rivalry, Christian themes including visiting Narnia (Ages 7-17) **Top 5 star reviews on Amazon**

The Second Book of Funtastic Adventures - David grandsons rescue their parents and sister from alien kidnappers. This is a follow on from the first book with many crazy, funny twists & turns before they succeed in their mission. Many of the characters from the first book show up again. (Ages 7-17)

The Adventures of Tiny the Bear - Tiny is a large grizzly from Lilliput so he is small in our world, but is very wise in helping children deal with a poor self image and bullying. A story that is cute and amusing; children & parents will love.

Printed by: FAITH PRINTING
4210 Locust Hill Road
Taylors SC 29687

Spiritual Armor

"Finally my brethren, be strong in the Lord, and in the power of His might.

Put on the whole armor of God, that ye may be able to stand against the wiles of the devil.

For we wrestle not against flesh and blood but against principalities, against powers, against the rulers of the darkness of this world, against spiritual wickedness in high places.

Wherefore take unto you the whole armor of God, that ye may be able to stand in the evil day, and having done all, to stand.

Stand therefore having your loins girded about with truth, and having on the breastplate of righteousness;

And your feet shod with the preparation of the gospel of peace;

Above all, taking the shield of faith, wherewith ye shall be able to quench the fiery darts of the wicked.

And take the helmet of salvation, and the sword of the Spirit, which is the word of God;

Praying always with all prayer and supplication in the Spirit, and watching thereunto with all perseverance and supplication for all saints;"

Ephesians 6:10-18 (KJV).

*This book is dedicated
to my two daughters, Faith and Lisa,
and to all God's children.*

Christian children!

The Bible tells us to be strong. That does not mean that you have to go and exercise with weights and become muscle-men. We could never become strong enough to defeat the devil and we cannot do God's will in our own strength.

The Bible says, "Be strong in the LORD and in the POWER of HIS MIGHT," not our might, but GOD'S

The way we become strong in the Lord is by putting on the SPIRITUAL ARMOR that God has provided. It is no good just putting on one or two pieces, but we are to put on the WHOLE armor of God.

We are in a battle and we wrestle against all the powers of darkness; which is the DEVIL and ALL HIS DEMONS. You usually can't see them, but you can see what they can do. In the same way we can't see God, but we can see what He can do.

Satan is very well equipped to do his dirty work and he has had PLENTY OF PRACTICE for he has been working since the beginning of the world. We must be covered in God's armor all the time if we are going to defeat him.

QUESTIONS FOR YOU TO ANSWER!

1. The Bible tells us to be _____.

2. How are we to be strong?   *Circle the correct answer.*

   a. In ourselves
   b. In the Lord
   c. Take vitamins
   d. Exercise with weights
   e. Join a health club

3. How are we to become strong in the Lord?

   By putting on the _____.

4. How many pieces of armor must we put on to defeat Satan and be victorious? _____.

5. Who are we in a battle against?   *Circle the correct answer.*

   a. The boy next door
   b. Our parents
   c. Bad people

   d. Our teachers
   e. The devil and his demons
   f. People that don't like us

6. Why is Satan well equipped to do his dirty work?

   He has had plenty of _____.

The devil will laugh at us if we try to beat him in our own strength …

… but

he gets REAL WORRIED when we have our armor on.

The armor is given to us, but WE MUST PUT IT ON *everyday.*

Children! It is essential for you as born again Christians to understand the need of wearing SPIRITUAL ARMOR for POWER in YOUR LIFE.

It is the ARMOR THAT IS MIGHTY, rather than YOU who wear it.

God's armor is a PERFECT FIT for children of every size and age.

It does not matter if you are weak, frail, timid, and little; once you are equipped in the POWER OF THE SPIRIT, you become MIGHTY.

In verses 11 and 13, the need to put on the WHOLE armor OF GOD is mentioned.

In verse 13, it says the reason we need the WHOLE armor is to withstand or STAND against the EVIL that attacks us now and in the EVIL day ahead.

1. What must we do to make the devil worried?

   _____.

2. How often should we wear our armor? *Circle the correct answer.*

   a. Once a year
   b. Sundays
   c. When our parents tell us to
   d. When we feel like it
   e. Every day

3. What does the spiritual armor give you? _____

4. Who will God's armor fit? _____

5. What happens to the weak, little, timid and frail after they put on the armor of God?   _____

6. How much armor are we to put on?   _____

It is important for us to know that the days we live in are EVIL. With all the nice things we often see around us, it's hard to believe that this is an evil day.

We think that if something is evil it must look bad, like a MONSTER or something, but it isn't always that way. Sin and evil can be wrapped up in PRETTY PACKAGES. If it wasn't, we wouldn't be so easily TEMPTED to do wrong.

God's armor enables us to stand and do all that is needed to keep on STANDING.

Many children do just enough so they can sit down and take it easy, but *remember* the Devil never takes a VACATION, so we can't EITHER. A good soldier is always on the lookout for the enemy.

LEARN TO SLEEP WITH YOUR ARMOR ON.

1. What kind of day do we live in?_____

2. Although sin and evil are ugly, how do they often look?

   _____

3. The devil wraps up sin in _____ _____ so we can be easily _____.

4. After we have stood against the devil and evil in battle what are we then to do? *Circle the correct answer.*

   a. Sit down
   b. Go on vacation
   c. Keep standing
   d. Take a break
   e. Lie down

5. What does the devil never do? _____

6. We must learn to _____ with our armor on.

8

The first piece of armor to put on, is the "BELT OF TRUTH."

This is the foundation garment (You could call it your spiritual underwear). It holds everything else together. You clip your sword, breast plate, gun, grenades, and other weapons to it.

You need to be grounded in the TRUTH (God's Word). You need to be convinced about the Word of God and learn to quote the Bible with conviction at all times, and especially when Satan tempts you.

When Jesus was tempted of the devil in Matthew, Chapter 4, He knew how to resist Satan by quoting God's Word. If the Son of God used that method to defeat the devil, then we can't expect to have victory unless we seriously use the SAME METHODS.

Jesus said: "If you continue in my Word then are you my disciples indeed; And you shall know the truth, and the truth shall make you free."
John 8:31-32.

If the truth shall make you free,

then lies,

(the opposite of truth)

shall bind you up.

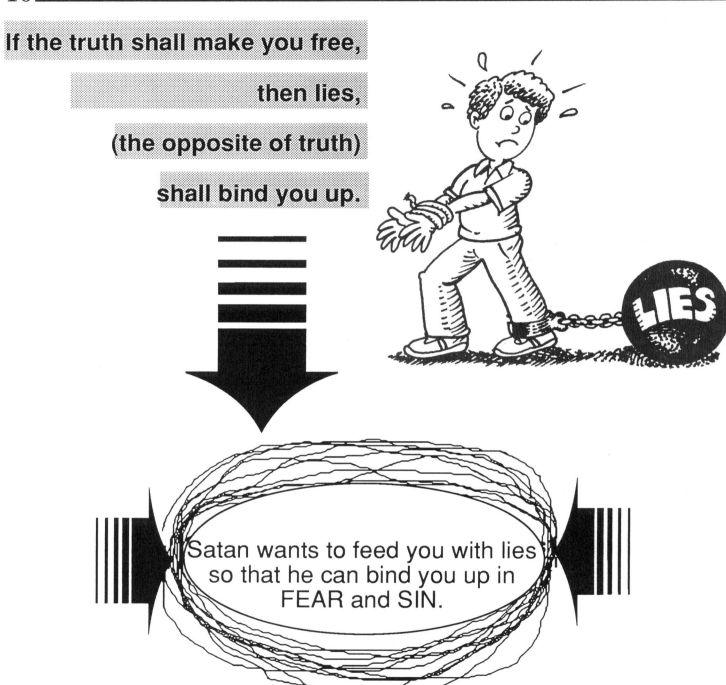

Satan wants to feed you with lies so that he can bind you up in FEAR and SIN.

If Satan can't get you to believe in lies, he will often try to get you to believe and trust in things that are true, but are not really THE TRUTH.

1. What is the first piece of armor we have to put on?_____

2. What is its function? or what does it do? _____

3. We know the purpose of the belt, but what is the **truth** that's mentioned? _____   _____

4. Jesus used a certain method in defeating the devil when He was tempted in the wilderness. We are to use the same method.

   What is it? _____

5. What does the **truth** make us?   _____

6. What will lies do to us? _____

7. If we are bound by Satan's lies, what will it produce in us?

   _____ and _____

- Satan may say you are only small and young so you can't expect God to use you too much.

   It may be TRUE that you are SMALL and YOUNG, but the armor God gives you is MIGHTY!

- Satan may say, "Don't witness to a crowd of kids because you are only one and they will all laugh at you."

   That's true, but the TRUTH is GREATER. "Greater is He that is in you than he that is in them," (I John 4:4).

- You may feel sick one day and Satan will tell you that you will just have to stay sick.

TRUE vs. ....

That may be true, but the TRUTH is that Jesus has healed you. "By Whose (Jesus) stripes <u>you were healed</u>," (I Peter 2:24). You can rise up and take your healing.

.... **TRUTH**

You can see from those examples that it is very important that you build your faith on the Truth of God's Word and not just feelings.

Feelings change, but
GOD'S WORD NEVER CHANGES

The Holy Spirit can only bring out of you that which HE has put in. If you are not serious about learning God's Truth from His Holy Word, it is hard for the Holy Spirit to use you. Even the Holy Spirit can't get something out of nothing.

> **Always remember the
> IMPORTANCE OF LEARNING AND
> BELIEVING GOD'S WORD.**

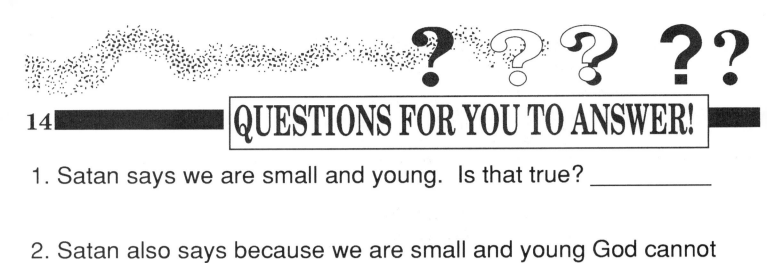

QUESTIONS FOR YOU TO ANSWER!

1. Satan says we are small and young. Is that true? _____

2. Satan also says because we are small and young God cannot use us. Is that true? _____

3. When you are around a lot of children that are not Christians and you want to tell them about Jesus but you are the only Christian, what should you do?   *Circle the correct answer.*

   a. Keep quiet
   b. Wait for more Christians to come
   c. Give your witness
   d. Don't risk embarrassment
   e. Wait for a better time

4. Why should you give your witness to a crowd of kids?

   a. Because you are the biggest
   b. Because you are the oldest
   c. Because greater is He that is in you than he that is in them
   d. To please your parents
   e. Because the church elders said you have to do it

5. What should we build our faith on?   *Circle the correct answer.*

   a. What people tell us   d. Wishful thinking
   b. Fairy stories   e. God's Word
   c. Our feelings   f. What we can see

6. What is it that never changes? _____

7. What is it that the Holy Spirit cannot do? _____

The next piece of armor is called the "BREASTPLATE of RIGHTEOUSNESS."

♥ ♥

The Breastplate is to protect your HEART.

♥ ♥

The Devil will always try to condemn you, or make you feel guilty or bad, especially if you mess up.

If you feel guilty in your heart ...

you will lose your peace with God ...

and you will not be any use ...

in battle.

I John 3:21

The wonderful thing about salvation is not that we just have our sins forgiven, but we are covered with a beautiful white robe of righteousness.

There was a famous hymn writer who wrote, *"JESUS my robe of righteousness, HIS beauty is, my GLORIOUS dress."* That means that all the GOOD things that Jesus did have been given to us and all the BAD things we have done have been taken away.

It is like being invited to a big party. You have the invitation, but you only have dirty old rags to wear. Jesus invites us to His party, but He also takes our dirty old rags off, gives us a bath in His blood to wash our sins away, and covers us with His BEAUTIFUL WHITE SHINING ROBE OF RIGHTEOUSNESS.

Righteousness is like standing before God, RICH and not poor.

 Jesus not only forgives us, but makes us FIT or ABLE for His kingdom.

When the Devil attacks us and points to all the sins and failures we have committed, we answer Him with, "Satan! Not only have I been forgiven, but I have also been given Jesus' righteousness (Goodness) as a GIFT, so YOU can't condemn me." THAT'S HAVING ON THE BREASTPLATE OF RIGHTEOUSNESS!

REMEMBER

♥ ♥ ♥ ♥ ♥ ♥ ♥ ♥ ♥ ♥ ♥ ♥ ♥ ♥ ♥ ♥ ♥ ♥ ♥ ♥

Make sure that you clip your Breastplate on to your Belt of Truth. That way, you will not get SLOPPY in your walk with the Lord and use the Breastplate for an excuse to sin.

We don't want to walk around all day feeling guilty because we are being condemned by the Devil.

We want to walk close to God and learn to have a . . .

**HOLY HATRED for SIN,
and a LOVE for PURITY and
OBEDIENCE.**

♥ ♥ ♥ ♥ ♥ ♥ ♥ ♥ ♥ ♥ ♥ ♥ ♥ ♥ ♥ ♥ ♥ ♥ ♥ ♥

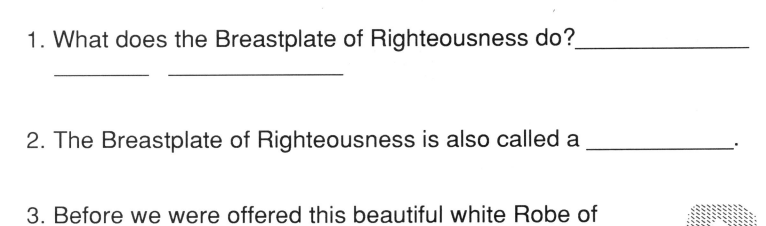

QUESTIONS FOR YOU TO ANSWER!

1. What does the Breastplate of Righteousness do? _____

_____   _____

2. The Breastplate of Righteousness is also called a _____.

3. Before we were offered this beautiful white Robe of Righteousness, what were we wearing? _____   _____

4. What does righteousness do for us? *Circle the correct answer.*

    a. Makes us poor, unworthy and humble
    b. Makes us proud, strong and clever
    c. Makes us rich, fit and able
    d. Makes us fearful, weak and wimpy

5. How do we get righteousness? *Circle the correct answer.*

    a. By working hard
    b. By being good
    c. By praying
    d. By accepting the gift by faith
    e. By reading the Bible

6. We are to learn to hate _____ and learn to love _____ and _____.

The next piece to wear are the "SHOES or BOOTS."

"Having your feet shod with the preparation of the gospel of peace."

As we are thinking about the army, let's think of boots rather than shoes. Shoes are made for walking, but boots are made for marching.

God has called all Christian children to *march into battle* in the POWER OF THE HOLY SPIRIT.

Christian boys and girls are not to just sit around and enjoy all the blessings of God and all the good things that their church may provide for them, but they are to *MARCH OUT INTO SATAN'S TERRITORY* (the world) and share the gospel — THE GOOD NEWS — with other children.

Perhaps you know kids in your neighborhood, or your school or at the sports field that need to make Jesus Lord of their lives and join God's army.

When you put on your boots that means you are willing to go out and tell others and not just sit at home and play, or watch T.V.

There are many children and Mom's and Dad's who are hurting and worried and unhappy, because they don't know what you know.

Most of them will not come knocking on your door asking you to tell them about Jesus.

That's why you have to:

"GO (with your boots on) TO ALL THE WORLD AND PREACH THE GOSPEL TO EVERYONE" (Mark 16:15).

Perhaps one day you will be a great evangelist, travelling all over the world preaching the gospel. RIGHT NOW YOU CAN START in your own neighbourhood learning how to be a witness for Jesus (Acts 1:8).

1. If shoes were made for_____ what are boots made for?

_____

2. Where are we to march? _____ and in what power?

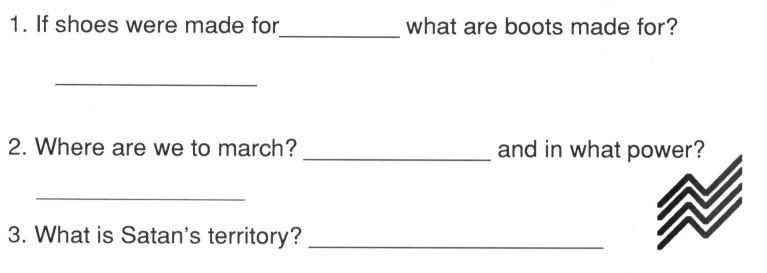

_____

3. What is Satan's territory? _____

4. Who are we to share the Good News with?   *Circle the correct answer.*

    a. Christians
    b. People we like
    c. Americans
    d. Everyone

    e. Foreigners
    f. Students
    g. People that don't like us
    h. Nobody

5. When we join God's army what are we expected to do?

Circle the correct answer.

    a. Sit at home
    b. Play
    c. Watch T.V.
    d. Wait

    e. Hang around
    f. Take a nap
    g. Go
    h. Take a bath

MORE QUESTIONS TO ANSWER!

6. Why are so many people worried, hurting and unhappy?

_____

7. Where do you start witnessing?   *Circle the correct answer.*

    a. Africa
    b. In church
    c. The nearest town
    d. Your own neighborhood
    e. A children's meeting

8. When should you start witnessing?   *Circle the correct answer.*

    a. When you are older
    b. After going to Bible college
    c. Tomorrow
    d. When your friends decide to witness
    e. Right now
    f. Never

THE SHIELD OF FAITH is a very important part of your armor.

Paul says: "ABOVE ALL, take the shield of faith."

If you go out without it you will be in DEAD TROUBLE. This is to protect you from the arrows, spears, missiles, and fiery darts that Satan will throw at you.

The shield is a SHIELD OF FAITH.

When the apostle Paul talked about the shield, he was thinking of the shields that the Roman soldiers used. They were very large, so that when they kneeled down it would cover their whole bodies. This is the way the Romans were successful in defeating their enemies.

They would march toward their foes, and when the enemy fired their arrows they would duck behind their shields. While the enemy were loading their bows, they would march forward again until they were right on top of them. Then they would get their swords out and kill them.

The arrows, spears, and fiery darts are doubts, fears, discouragements, and temptations that Satan hurls at you.

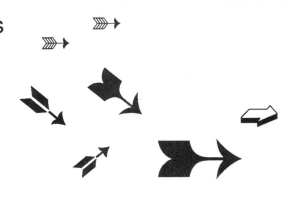

If he can get you into unbelief and doubt, he has you conquered.

We are to learn to ... LIVE BY FAITH, WALK BY FAITH AND STAND IN FAITH.

When everything seems to be going wrong and nothing is working out, when the people we have witnessed to don't seem to be interested, when we feel God does not seem to care about us anymore, then we LIFT UP OUR SHIELD OF FAITH and recognize where all these attacks are coming from.

When we lift up our shield all the missiles that Satan throws will just bounce off and **we will be VICTORIOUS.**

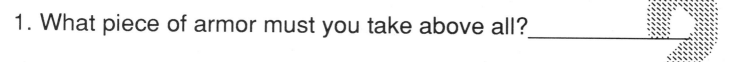

1. What piece of armor must you take above all?_____

2. What are the arrows, spears, missiles, and fiery darts that Satan hurls at us? _____

3. When all these doubts, fears, discouragements, and temptations come against us, what must we lift up? _____

4. What are we to walk, live and stand in? *Circle the correct answer.*

    a. Fear
    b. Feelings
    c. Our reasoning
    d. Faith
    e. Our ideas

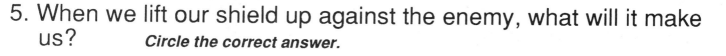

5. When we lift our shield up against the enemy, what will it make us? *Circle the correct answer.*

    a. Sick
    b. Wealthy
    c. Proud
    d. Victorious
    e. Humble

THE HELMET OF SALVATION
is to wear on your head.

It is to protect your mind from *STINKING THINKING.*

The Bible says that when we are born again, we are given a NEW MIND even the MIND OF CHRIST.

Ephesians 4:23, I Corinthians 2:16

Satan want's to hit you in the head and mess up your mind.

He does it by putting bad, mean, selfish, and impure thoughts in your head. He will keep attacking, to try to get you to do lots of things without thinking. If he succeeds, you will do foolish and dangerous things that will get you into trouble.

You must
PUT ON YOUR HELMET

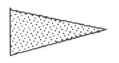

Yes you must PUT ON YOUR HELMET.
Another way the Bible says it is,
"LET THE MIND OF CHRIST BE IN YOU."
(Philippians 2:5).

It does not just happen, you have to *LET* it happen.

PUT off the old man *(our old ways of thinking and behaving)* and PUT on the NEW *(Christ's way of thinking and behaving, Ephesians 4:22-24).* Think of the PUTTING ON and the PUTTING OFF like going out in the cold.

When you go out in the cold you PUT ON your coat, and when you come in again you PUT OFF your coat. Putting off the old, putting on the new, and putting on your armor, should become a SPIRITUAL HABIT for you.

I like to think of the HELMET OF SALVATION as having EARPHONES attached to it. This keeps you in contact with your CAPTAIN (Jesus). You are receiving HIS instructions so then you can't hear the Devil.

The HELMET definitely protects you from SATAN'S LIES.

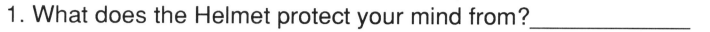

1. What does the Helmet protect your mind from?_____

2. What is the mind called that you have been given?
   Circle the correct answer.
   a. A clever mind
   b. A new mind
   c. A lazy mind
   d. A carnal mind

3. You must put on your _____ and let the mind of _____ be in you.

4. What must we put off? _____

5. What should become a habit to us? *Circle the correct answer.*

   a. Eating
   b. Putting on our socks
   c. Putting on our armor
   d. School work
   e. Sleeping
   f. Putting up with people

6. What does the Helmet have attached to it? _____

7. What are the earphones for? *Circle the correct answer.*

   a. Keeping our ears warm
   b. Listening to the devil
   c. Receiving God's instructions
   d. Listening to rock music

The SWORD of the SPIRIT is for ATTACK not DEFENSE

The other armor has been given to protect you. Although the boots were made to enable you to march into battle, they still protect your feet. The Sword is for ATTACK NOT DEFENSE. A real army is one that attacks the enemy. If we are in this world just to defend our faith, then we will be defeated.

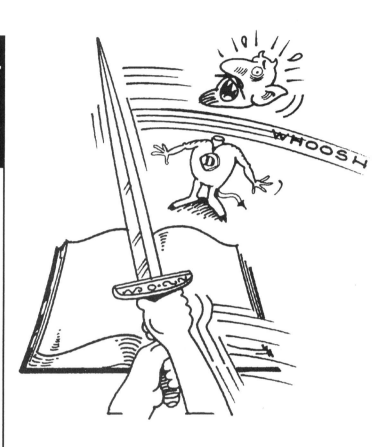

We have the greatest power in the universe
THE SWORD OF THE SPIRIT
which is
THE WORD OF GOD.

The sword is not given to put into a sheath but to wield, cut, thrust, and pierce the enemy.

__The Word of God is given to us to deal with every problem and to answer every attack from Satan.__

Satan will often talk to us through:
- people
- radio
- television
- books
- newspapers
- movies
- magazines

We need to recognize Satan's words and attack them with
THE WORD OF GOD.

REMEMBER ... Jesus dealt with the Devil by using the Word of God when he quoted the scripture:

"Thus says the Lord" ... "It is Written."

 You must *LEARN THE WORD OF GOD* and many scripture verses, to enable you to answer the questions and attacks that you will experience.

Like sword fighting, the more you do it, the more expert you become and the more you use God's Word, the better you will do it. You cannot grow on your own, but you do *GROW IN THE LORD*; if you obey and *USE HIS WORD* (Ephesians 4:15). God also wants you to grow with others. That is why it is important that you have spiritual brothers and sisters who can encourage you in the battles ahead ••••••• **You can't make it alone.**

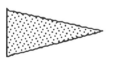

1. What is the Sword used for? *Circle the correct answer.*

    a. To defend yourself
    b. To cut up your food
    c. To attack with
    d. To sharpen pencils

2. The greatest power in the universe is? *Circle the correct answer.*

    a. Satan
    b. Nuclear bomb
    c. Angels
    d. Superman

    e. President of the United States
    f. The Sword of the Spirit
    g. Russia
    h. Star Wars

3. Give three ways Satan can talk to you. _____, _____,
    and _____

4. You must learn the _____ _____ _____ to answer the
    attacks and questions that you will experience.

5. What are you to grow in? _____ _____

Lastly —

> > > >

In Matthew 26:41, Jesus said to the disciples "Watch and pray that ye enter not into temptation" … We are not told just to pray, but to **"WATCH"** and pray. In Ephesians 6:18, we are told to WATCH with all perseverance.

Persevere **means you don't give up, or lose interest, but you stick with it. To persevere means that we keep on watching, not just for a few moments, but all the time. We keep on doing it until we have achieved our goals.**

WATCH and PRAY

In the army, soldiers have to do guard duty. That is really a WATCH. They are called guards or sentries. They either guard the army camp, or the weapons and ammunition.

says "Friend" then they have to give the secret password, or identify themselves

Remember, we are in God's army and we must always be on the watch for our enemy SATAN. We must not let him get past our defenses. We are not only to watch out for ourselves by wearing our armor, but watch out for our brothers and sisters, by staying ON GUARD.

Some of the guards or sentries are given little sheds to stand in. Every so often they march up and down protecting that which they are put in charge of. You may have heard of the expression "Who goes there, friend or foe?" If someone

QUESTIONS FOR YOU TO ANSWER!

1. We are told not just to pray, but to _____ also.

2. What does persevere mean? _____

3. What are soldiers in the army sometimes called?

Circle the correct answer.

a. Rookies
b. Veterans
c. Guards or sentries
d. Commandos

4. Soldiers have to guard the camp and weapons etc. Who do we have to be on guard for apart from ourselves? _____

5. Who are we to be on the watch for? _____ And what will he try to get past? _____

WATCH and PRAY

Watch and "PRAY" this is more than just saying a few prayers before you go to bed. It is more than just being asked to give thanks at dinner or made to pray at a meeting. It says in Ephesians 6:18 praying "ALWAYS." "How can you do that?" you might ask. "You have to do other things, you can't just be praying all the time!"

It means being in an ATTITUDE OF PRAYER. That means that you are always ready to pray and you pray at every opportunity. You may be walking along and you start praising God and praying for His will to be done. It is getting up in the morning and asking God to use you this day for His Glory.

• • • • • • • • •

> LORD, USE MY LIFE TO GLORIFY YOU...

Many children just ask God to give them a good time and give them the things that they want. If that's mostly what you pray about, then your prayers are just selfish ones and are not the real prayers that God delights to hear.

Although God wants to bless us and gives us nice things and nice times …

He wants us to put Him first and be WILLING to REALLY SERVE HIM.

If we seek to do that, God will take care of us AND BLESS US, Matthew 6:33).

Satan loves to hear children whine, gripe, and complain. It is music to his ears.

If you learn to PRAISE AND PRAY, it gives the Devil an ear ache; he can't stand it.

If you pray in the Spirit (praying in other tongues), that's even worse for the Devil because he can't understand what you are saying so he can't challenge your prayers

The only thing he can say is that praying in tongues is silly and you are just making it up. The Devil has made lots of Christians believe that. Many are too proud to do what seems a foolish thing; like PRAYING IN OTHER TONGUES. Some children cannot see the point in this kind of prayer.

Often we don't quite know how best to pray for difficult problems, but that's when praying in tongues really helps us out. Although our mind may not understand what to pray for, our spirit does. We are speaking MYSTERIES to God, (I Corinthians 14:2).

Always
REMEMBER

♥ ♥

… to pray for others, especially those who you know are not yet saved.

When you witness to them, keep on praying for them. Pray against Satan, who blinds their minds and keeps them his prisoners.

You have been called of God, to rescue and set the captives free.

♥ ♥

QUESTIONS FOR YOU TO ANSWER!

1. Write in your own words the difference between saying prayers and PRAYING. _____

   _____

2. What are selfish prayers? _____

3. What are real prayers? _____

4. What will God do if we put Him first and be willing to serve Him?
   Circle the correct answer.

   a. Punish us
   b. Make us famous
   c. Make us miserable
   d. Take care of and bless us

5. What does Satan love to hear us do? _____, _____,

   and _____.

6. What do we do to the Devil if we praise God and pray?
   _____

7. When you pray in tongues, why does it frustrate the Devil? _____
   _____

8. Satan tries to make Christians believe that Praying in Tongues is
   _____.

9. When you witness to people, you are to keep on _____
   for them.

CHAPTER ONE — Page 2

1. Strong
2. In the Lord
3. Spiritual armor

4. Six
5. The Devil and his demons
6. Practice

CHAPTER ONE — Page 5

1. Have our armor on
2. Every day
3. Power

4. People of every size and age
5. You become mighty
6. The whole armor

CHAPTER ONE — Page 7

1. Evil
2. Pretty
3. Pretty packages — tempted

4. Keep standing
5. Take a vacation
6. Sleep

CHAPTER TWO — Page 11

1. The belt of truth
2. It holds everything else together
3. God's Word

4. Quoting God's Word
5. Free
6. Bind you up
7. Fear and sin

CHAPTER TWO — Page 14

1. Yes
2. No
3. Give your witness

4. Because greater is He that is in you than he that is in them
5. God's Word
6. God's Word
7. Get something out of nothing

CHAPTER THREE — Page 18

1. Protects your heart
2. White robe
3. Filthy rags

4. Makes us rich, fit and able
5. By accepting the gift by faith
6. Sin — purity and obedience

CHAPTER FOUR — Page 21 and 22

1. Walking — marching
2. Into battle — The power of the Spirit
3. The world

4. Everyone
5. Go
6. They don't know what we know
7. Your own neighborhood
8. Right now

CHAPTER FIVE — Page 25

1. The shield of faith
2. Doubts, fears, discouragements and temptations
3. Our shield of faith

4. Faith
5. Victorious

CHAPTER SIX— Page 29

1. Stinking thinking
2. A new mind
3. Helmet — Christ

4. Our old man
5. Putting on our armor
6. Earphones
7. Receiving God's instructions

CHAPTER SEVEN — Page 33

1. To attack
2. The Sword of the Spirit
3. People, radio, T.V., books, newspapers, magazines, movies

4. Word of God
5. The Lord

and more ANSWERS

CHAPTER EIGHT — Page 36

1. Watch
2. Keep on
3. Guards or sentries
4. Our brothers and sisters
5. Satan — our defenses
6. Sin — purity and obedience

CHAPTER EIGHT— Page 40

1. ――――――――
2. Praying for things we want
3. Praying for others
4. Take care of and bless us
5. Whine, gripe and complain
6. Give him an ear ache
7. He doesn't know what we are saying
8. stupid
9. praying

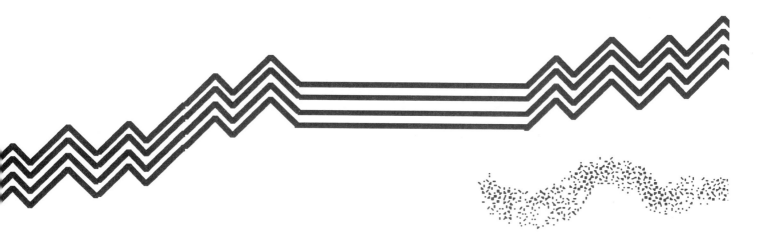

RAISING A GENERATION OF
ANOINTED CHILDREN AND YOUTH

ONE-DAY TRAINING SEMINAR

Equipping Parents, Youth Pastors,
Sunday School Teachers and Children's Workers

The churches in your area can experience one of these dynamic seminars. Author and speaker David Walters imparts a fresh vision and anointing to parents and to those who work with children and youth. Walters says:

Children do not have a baby or junior Holy Spirit!

Children are baptized in the Holy Spirit to do much more than play, be entertained or listen to a few moral object lessons!

The average church-wise child can be turned around and set on fire for God!

Christian teenagers do not have to surrender to peer pressure — they can become the peers!.

FOR INFORMATION ON CHILDREN'S CRUSADES
OR FAMILY AND TEACHER'S SEMINARS,
CALL OR WRITE:

GOOD NEWS FELLOWSHIP MINISTRIES
220 SLEEPY CREEK ROAD
MACON, GA 31210

PHONE (478) 757-8071
FAX (478) 757-0136